Grip, Grin and Greet

By Luann Alemao

The POPular guide for success at work or play

Copyright©2002 Luann Alemao
Cedar Falls, IA 50613
All rights reserved.
No part of this book may be reproduced or transmitted in any form or by any means, electronic or mechanical, including photocopying, recording or by any information storage and retrieval system, without permission in writing from the publisher.

Publication #8708

Printed in the United States of America by:

G & R Publishing Company
507 Industrial Street
Waverly, IA 50677
800-383-1679
gandr@gandrpublishing.com
http://www.cookbookprinting.com

Introduction

I wrote this book because of several significant events in my life. As a child, although I didn't fully understand this at the time, I learned that customer service and hospitality start at home! I saw this in action daily as I grew up. My family always embraced the fact that we had a new baby in the family or new neighbors. These were reasons to celebrate: to host an event where everyone got together to meet the new neighbor or baby with a coffee cake or muffins. It was just what you did!

As I grew up and became an adult I remembered and lived by this philosophy. But, after college graduation when I became a high school Family and Consumer Science teacher (Home Economics), I was truly awakened by the social skills of teenagers in my classes. Or, maybe I should say, their lack of these skills. It wasn't just because of the awkwardness of being a teenager either. It seemed they lacked knowledge of interpersonal skills. I saw that they were minus a big plus in the world of work after high school. I set out on a mission and had no idea where it would take me.

After I married, life's circumstances took me 2,000 miles from my home on the West Coast to the Midwest. This came as a real culture shock to me. However, I noticed the people in the Midwest seemed to have no fear of strangers. They welcomed anyone into their homes and businesses. For instance, when I attended my first cattle branding, I recognized many kinds of hospitality. I knew nothing about Wyoming cowboys and their way of life. So I watched as the women at the cattle branding bustled about in the kitchen preparing the food for more than 200 people. I watched as neighbors came from 60 miles around to help with the branding. These shows of hospitality amazed me. I felt a little awkward with my camera ready, my makeup applied and my Capri pants with matching tennies, but these folks were as hospitable as a farmer to a stray cat that finds his way straight to the farm. I was accepted, even being a California girl, as the new Midwesterner.

Life's circumstances also led me to travel quite a bit, sometimes out of the country. As a people watcher and observer, I was fascinated with the relationships I saw between business colleagues and family members. The importance of relationships really hit me when I understood the global perspective and its relevance. You can be in Europe in less than 8 hours, among a new culture where you're instantly a neighbor, not that far from your home country or continent. I took that insight back to the high school classroom and the teenagers that I taught. I wanted to help them understand that relationships are what matters, the treatment of people, not where you live or where you are from.

As life happened, two more major events led to this book. The first was becoming a parent—that God giving blessing. The other was adversity—a taste of my faith being put to the test. When my husband was diagnosed with a brain tumor, my world crumbled beneath me. But, because of these two events, my husband and I learned to give and receive true hospitality. We learned the graciousness of our community. We experienced the many blessings and kindnesses of the people that God puts in our lives.

My husband still has residual disabilities and that really encouraged me to write this book. I watched how the world reacts to him and to us as a couple and family. I want to help those who have disabilities and those of us who live in communities with people with disabilities. I have devoted a chapter in the book on that topic.

As a result of adversity, love and compassion, I've written this book to help people be more successful at work and at play while creating stronger relationships.

                                          Luann Alemao,
                                          Summer 2002

Acknowledgments

It is with heartfelt gratitude to the following people that this book was written,

My parents, who always believed in me

My husband, who is a constant inspiration

the community in which I live that has always provided a support system for my goals;
and anyone who has touched my life in any way, this book is for you.
God Bless you!

Preface

As a parent, teacher, speaker and trainer in the field of relationship management for 22 years, I wrote this book at the request and encouragement of mentors, family, colleagues and friends. Moving and traveling around the country, abroad and within the states, made me realize how global we truly are. Now that I am a Midwesterner living among the soybeans and corn, I've had a revelation! We, as people, are much like popcorn. We are great "kernels," just plain and unseasoned. Once we add the seasonings—the education, experiences, books, manners and etiquette, relationships with people–globally and in our own back yard—we become seasoned and develop flavor as people. We become magnets for others because our seasonings have refined and matured. Like popcorn, we are enriched with seasonings. "It's the little seasonings that make the big difference."

Grip, Grin and Greet
A POPular guide for success in work and play

Table of Contents

Introduction
Acknowledgments
Preface

Chapter 1- The Grin-Introductions To All 1
The 60 Second Impression 1
    The Grin–Introductions 2
    The Grip-Handshakes 6
    Introductions to People with Disabilities 8

Chapter 2-Global Do's and Taboos 11

Chapter 3-Correspondence 13
Thank You Notes 14
E-Mail and FAX 16
When to RSVP 18
Words that invite 19

Chapter 4-POPular Phone Use 21
Cell Phone Use 22
Telephone Tactics 23
Marvelous Message Taking 25

Chapter 5-When and How to Use Business Cards 27
Business Cards 28

**Chapter 6-Jetiquette-
Trains, Planes and Automobiles** 31
Jetiquette 32
Auto Travel 33
Train Travel 34
Tips for the Traveler 35

Chapter 7-Manners at Play 37
At the Symphony, Concert or Play 38
Patriotism... 39
At the Movies.. 40
The Sport of It 41

Chapter 8-Manners for Many Occasions 43
Compliments 44
Speech 45
Tips For Speech.. 46
Conversation Starters and Stoppers................... 47
Remembering Names 49
Sympathy Etiquette 50

Chapter 9-Office Manners 51
Networking 52
The Bully 55
Pregnancy Protocol 56
The Office Party 57
Be Social and Suave 58
Party Queues... 60
What to Wear to the Party 62

Chapter 10-Dress for the Interview 63
What should be included in a job
interview wardrobe for women and men 64
Five Winning Wardrobe Wonders....................... 66

Chapter 11-Present Protocol or Gift Glitches 67
Present Protocol or Gift Glitches 68
The Last Wrap on Gifts 70

Chapter 12-Entertaining 101 71
Entertaining 101 72
Toasting 74
Guidelines for the Perfect Toast 74
Wine Serving and Selection 75
Wine and Food 77
How to Handle Disaster Dilemmas 78

Chapter 13-Delightful Dining 79
Tips on Tipping 82
How Do We Eat It? 83
Terms on the Menu 85

Chapter 14-Hospitality 89
Some Hit Party Ideas and Menus 90
Cookie Exchange 91
Trim the Tree 92
Chili Con Carne 94
Bountiful Blessings 96
Celebrate Your Heritage Party 97
Valentine Party or Couple's Dinner Party 98
Cheezy Beefy Strudel 100
Cherries Jubilee 102
New Year's Eve Jammie Party 103
Belgian Waffles 105

x

Chapter 1

The Grin Introductions to All

The 60-Second Impression
"The smile is an inexpensive way to improve your looks."

As I read and travel, the most important strategy I've noticed in developing rapport with people is a genuine smile, a touch and repeating someone's name. Nothing speaks to us more than someone who calls us by name and gives us a handshake or a warm gesture of "glad you're here" by lightly brushing our shoulder or elbow. Simple gestures such as this and offering a simple "good morning" to co-workers, neighbors and others during your day can create verbal sunshine.

The Grin–Introductions

"You can get everything you want in life if you just help enough people get what they want."
Zig Zigler

- **Introductions** should be performed in any group of people who are new or unfamiliar with one another.

- **Wear name tags** on the right side.

- **Don't make people look for your name tags** by sticking it on your briefcase or handbag. Keep it in full view for maximizing your relationships. That also means wearing the name tag on your jacket and not underneath on your dress or shirt.

- **Use the individual's name** and make eye contact while engaged in the introduction. Use their name in conversation. This will cement their name quicker in your mind. Nothing is more important than eye contact with anyone. Make sure you connect and that your eyes aren't roaming around looking for someone more interesting.

- **When you join right hands to shake**, it's easier to see name tags. Wear your brooch or insignia pin on the right side as well. The pin can create a beginning conversation with your new acquaintance. For example: "I see your pin. I'm a Toastmaster too"; or "I was noticing your brooch. It's very unique."

- **Place the pin or the name tag** about 5 inches down from your shoulder. It is easier to build the rapport with the person you are conversing with if the name tag is in view.

- **Introduce yourself** with the name you want people to remember you by. If you use a nickname, or if you are introducing yourself to children, use your title, then last name. For example: "Hello, Emily I'm Mrs. Alemao. I know your mom from work."

- **It is permissible** for women to initiate a handshake. In business etiquette, gender specific does not apply. If no one else does so, women should absolutely initiate a handshake.

- **Introduce yourself** if no one initiates it first. It could be that people have forgotten your name and feel awkward. Prevent those moments from happening. Be prepared to introduce yourself and don't wait for someone else to do it for you.

- **The client or guest is** <u>always</u> mentioned first. The customer is always the guest of honor and should be introduced to the individual, whether it is the CEO, president, or the janitorial staff.

- **Use honorifics or titles** (Mr., Ms., Judge, etc.) in introductions especially if the person is old enough to be your parent. Titles are used professionally, but typically omitted in social etiquette situations. For example: Dr. or Judge is usually dropped, but some individuals still insist on their titles.

- **Children should be instructed** to always call adults by their title and last name. Adults are to lead here and say, "Please call me 'Marie'," or "Call me Mr. Jones." Call people old enough to be your parents by their last name and title such as: Mr. Johnson, Mrs. Thomas, or Ms. Wilson, unless they indicate otherwise.

- **The adult should set the standard** on what they want to be called. This shows a matter of respect and no one should be so presumptuous as to call someone by their last name only or abbreviate a name (Andy when the name is Andrew) without permission.

- **When referring to someone old enough to be your parent,** use their title and last name.

- **When an adult or professional gives permission for first name basis,** that is your cue to use their first name to acknowledge them.

POP Points of Performance

When to speak
A Good Conversationalist is usually well read. To be successful in any industry you need to be a charismatic communicator with good work habits, good people skills and have a supply of energy. Reading one book a month in your area of expertise will keep you abreast, current and interesting to converse with.

- **In written business correspondence**, refer to someone by the last name in the heading if you have never met them. For example: a letter is addressed to Mr. Smith, not Doug, if you and he have never met or talked.

- **Stand up** when offering a handshake, unless you're physically unable.

- **If you are the introducer**, give others a little biography about the individual. It helps to build conversation and lasting business relationships.

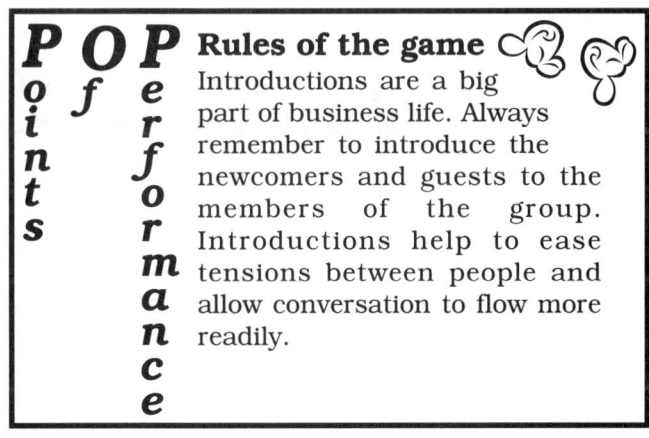

POP Points of Performance — Rules of the game

Introductions are a big part of business life. Always remember to introduce the newcomers and guests to the members of the group. Introductions help to ease tensions between people and allow conversation to flow more readily.

The Grip–Handshakes

Shaking hands is nearly a universal greeting and dates back to 2800 B.C. in Egypt. The handshake was first established as a gesture of goodwill. Weapons were usually worn on the right hip or carried in the right pocket. When you extended your right hand you were revealing you were without weapons and the handshake evolved.

The handshake establishes the initial rapport that is so vital and needed for grounding effective relationship management. A handshake can express control, professionalism and hospitality. It's the single most important "no cost" tool to organizations and individuals.

"To offer one's hand is that proof of goodwill; it should be received with respect and gratitude."
St. John Baptist de la Salle

- **Shaking hands is permissible** upon meeting and leaving an individual. This is the single most important rapport builder in a professional and social situation. Many a first impression is grounded by this simple, but effective, greeting. Many employers have shared with me that they develop a strong first impression by the handshake.

- **Shake web to web.** When joining hands, make sure as you hook thumbs, that you insert your hand far enough to shake web to web of the hand. Otherwise, you'll receive a wimpy handshake with only fingertips touching. On the other hand, you don't have to offer the power-gripper handshake and cause pain with your squeeze. Be aware. Your client or the other person could be affected by arthritis or have a hand wound, and their hand is not a place to inflict pain.

- **A 2 to 3 second handshake** pumping is sufficient. Count to yourself. Count quietly to yourself, however, or the other person will think you're really kooky!

- **Offer a light touch** on someone's elbow if you have built previous rapport with the individual. Use your left hand to grab the person's elbow as you are shaking hands. This shows established rapport building and a previous relationship has occurred. However, refrain from patting the top of the person's hand while engrossed in a handshake. This movement is especially condescending and patronizing between professionals.

- **When engaging in a handshake,** especially with an older family member, such as 85-year-old Uncle Joe or 75-year-old Grandma Martha, they may pat the top of your hand as a nurturing loving gesture.

- **Be aware of the "wimpy" handshake.** This is the handshake that just involves the finger tips and isn't a full web to web shake. It can leave people with the impression that you aren't credible, or confident. Women are often guilty of this one. Beware, ladies!

Introductions to People with a Disability

There are over 20 million people with disabilities in our nation. If we think about it, we probably know someone with a disability through work, family or community. We may even have encountered our own short-term disability involving crutches or a cast. We are all what are called "tab" people—"temporarily able bodied." It's just a matter of time before we encounter our own disability. Consideration and kindness should be the result of all encounters with all individuals that you meet.

"Kindness is a language the deaf can hear and the blind can see."
Author Unknown

- **Put people first** before the disability. Use phrases such as: person who is blind, rather than blind person; person with disablement, rather than disabled person, etc.

- **Greet and introduce yourself** just as you would to others. Extend your hand to the person, but if he/she has non-functioning limbs, you could lightly touch their shoulder to establish rapport. If the person is not receptive, you've been hospitable.

- **Make eye contact**. If an individual is in a wheel chair or mobility cart, you can lean over to introduce yourself. Acknowledgment and eye contact are important to all. However, refrain from perching yourself on their wheelchair, tousling their hair, etc.

- **Speak directly to the individual**. If they need assistance speaking or interpretating, a caregiver will be able to assist. Don't assume that someone isn't capable of speaking or being understood.

- **Ask individuals if they need assistance** with a door, getting into the elevator, handling books, papers, or packages. If they need assistance, they will generally let you know.

- **Be careful about making assumptions** concerning people who have a disability. Don't tag on another disability. For instance, people with a speech dysfunction often are interpreted as not being able to hear or see as well. We sometimes want to speak slower to an individual who is blind or speak louder to someone who is in a wheelchair, because we assume that if there is one disability there must be more.

- **Use proper vocabulary**. Saying "confined to a wheelchair" sounds harsh and unkind. A wheelchair gives them more mobility, so it's not confinement. "Uses a wheelchair" is a better way to describe it. Saying words like "crippled" or "retarded" are not permissible and are very unkind if someone has a disablement.

- **If children have a disablement**, be sure to also acknowledge them if you meet them on a family outing. People come first. It's permissible and hospitable to touch them, (shake hands if they are of junior high age) and extend a gesture of hello. Comments such as a "Hello", "I hope you are having a good day", or "It's good to see you" are sufficient.

- **Don't be so sensitive** with your speech that you're hesitant about saying "see you later" to your blind friend or "got to run" to your friend who uses a walking assistive device or has an artificial limb.

Chapter 2

Global Do's and Taboos

We are definitely a global society with a rich heritage and many cultures. One of my favorite sayings is "Think local, but act global." Be aware of your business associates, friends and family that you travel to visit whether it's for business or for pleasure. I learned, in meeting a gentleman from Bangladesh, how important it was for him to greet me correctly. He was very concerned about saying the right words to a woman and being unoffensive. He had attended a seminar of mine and was actually the tech person for the room. He had brought a book to read, but I noticed as I gave my presentation that he wasn't reading; he was soaking in everything I said. It was important to him to be respectful of the country and its protocol. We all should be so aware!

Global Do's and Taboos

"Good manners are made up of petty sacrifices."
Ralph Waldo Emerson

- **Do as the Romans do** is safe protocol. It's up to you as a visitor to the country to research and discover the cultural mores and acceptances so you make the fewest faux pas possible.

- **Be prepared to build relationships**. Many cultures need warm-up time. People in some cultures want a relationship, not just the "deal" of business in a hurry to sign the contract. It may take several meetings before business is actually brought to the table. Many cultures need warm up time before the contract is signed.

- **Be an informed visitor**. Know something about the history of the country or culture, its famous people, entertainers, artists, historians and monuments. People in other cultures will find it flattering when you've done your homework.

- **You might want to buy a guidebook** to give yourself more expertise. I recommend the Frommers or Fodors travel guides, available at your local bookstore.

- **"This is how we do it in the States"** probably won't fly with some nations. You are on their stomping grounds and should abide by their protocol.

Chapter 3

Correspondence

The written word has more impact than anything else, according to experts. Nothing can highlight a day more than the thank you note that arrives on your desk or table. Many of our great leaders, such as Kennedy and Roosevelt, knew the power of the written word. Your written word can add wind to someone's sails and add verbal sunshine to their day.

Thank You Notes

"Always remember that it is better to give than to receive; besides you don't have to write thank you notes."

- **Thank you notes can be sent** for kind gestures, gifts, favors and acts of kindness. (If you are unsure if a thank you note is required, defer on the safe side and send one.)

- **Never ask for a favor** in a note. (This is the greatest faux pas of thank you notes; it's pure and simple thanks.)

- **Send within 24 hours**—that is when a thank you is most appreciated. (This will become habit in the future this way.)

- **Wedding thank yous** can be sent within 3 months of the wedding. Brides and grooms can have envelopes addressed ahead of time and write the note together.

- **Get children in the habit of writing thank yous.** If you start them early, it will become a habit in adult life. Nothing pleases relatives or friends more than a child who shows appreciation for gifts or kind gestures they receive. Children can send a thank you as early as age 3. I started this by having the children draw picture thank yous for their gifts. I wrote the message that they recited to me on their drawing.

Chapter 3 - Correspondence

- **Keep a thank you free** from spelling errors. It spoils the message when you are trying to read through scribbles or scratch outs.

- **Make them hand written.** An exception: A business thank you can be computer generated, but a hand-written note is always acceptable.

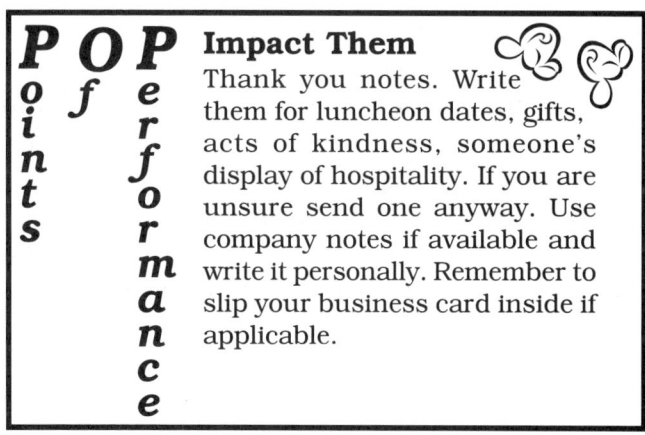

P O P **Impact Them**
o f **e**
i **r**
n **f** Thank you notes. Write
t **o** them for luncheon dates, gifts,
s **r** acts of kindness, someone's
    m display of hospitality. If you are
    a unsure send one anyway. Use
    n company notes if available and
    c write it personally. Remember to
    e slip your business card inside if
         applicable.

E-mail and FAX

As we delve more into the computer and technology age, we need to realize that television didn't replace radio and E-mails and the FAX machine won't replace the person-to-person satisfaction you receive from talking directly with someone. Using technology has its benefits and glitches, just as any other mode of communication. It's best to use it wisely with consideration and courtesy.

- **Use E-mail as a follow-up** to correspondence, for confirmation and inquiries.

- **Avoid using E-mail** as a formal thank you note. It's very impersonal.

- **Personal information** should always be relayed person to person or voice-to-voice (such as divorces, deaths, severe or terminal illnesses, etc.).

- **Avoid profanity or off-color remarks**. It doesn't speak highly of you as a professional to relay profanity or off-color jokes to co-workers or friends.

- **Use upper and lower case letters** and not all capital letters. A message in all capitals looks as though you are shouting at your recipient.

Chapter 3 - Correspondence

- **Save personal information** for voice-to-voice or person-to-person. A faxed message is much like a postcard, anyone is subject to reading it.

- **Fiery e-mails** are usually a mistake. Would you say it in person? Probably not! Give yourself time to cool down and don't send it.

> *Remember the Hierarchy of Most Effective Communications*
>
> Harvard Business School
>
> 1. Face to Face meetings
> 2. Phone calls
> 3. Voice-mail calls
> 4. E-mail

P ***O*** ***P*** **Respond to**
o *f* ***e*** **business letters**
i   ***r*** **within 4 days.**
n   ***f*** If the matter is less
t   ***o*** crucial you may respond
s   ***r*** within 2 weeks.
       m
       a
       n
       c
       e

When to RSVP

"Something so simple, something so often forgotten."
Luann Alemao,
Image, etiquette and leadership expert

I will always remember my cousin's wedding and her sit-down dinner reception where 25-35 people didn't notify my aunt and uncle that their plans had changed and they were not able to attend. The family took home rosemary chicken and ate it for days after the wedding. A simple note or phone call to decline or notify a change of plans could have made it so simple to avoid the nuisance and unnecessary expense.

- **Be timely with your response**. Always respond within 2-3 days after receiving an invitation. It helps the host or hostess plan accordingly.

- **If you need to cancel an engagement,** try to give the host enough notice. With a large function, such as a wedding or reception, 20-30 cancellations can make a huge difference in food preparation.

- **When you send an invitation,** try to avoid saying "regrets only". You may never know if the guest even received the invitation. This can be a confusing way to invite guests.

- **If you canceled your reservation** but plans changed and you can now attend the function, inform the responsible party. It's just plain good manners to say, "I'm coming," or "I'm not coming."

- **When mailing invitations,** give them a personal touch by handwriting them. Computer labels can be used for company business and correspondence. It is considered inappropriate to use them on wedding or party invitations.

Words that Invite

It's helpful to be able to recognize and interpret the words used on an invitation. They refer to the dress, the climate of the affair and are a good indicator of what to expect.

"the pleasure of your company"
a more formal affair

"Are you available"
casual affair

"Please join us"
very casual affair

Chapter 4

POPular Phone Use

The cell phone has been called the cigarette of the 60's because thousands of people own phones. We now have created restaurants with cell phone use rooms and cell free areas in which to dine. With the work environment changing, it's still important and not old-fashioned to say: "People come before technology."

You may have seen the bumper sticker that says "Hang up and drive." For many people the cell phone is required, but it needs to be used responsibly. When you're driving or talking face to face with someone that is your priority. The cell phone should become less of an irritant for others.

Cell Phone Use

- **Turn the cell phone off** at the table or during meals. If you don't have time for an uninterrupted meal, it's best to schedule it for another time or tell your guest you may have to excuse yourself for a call. However, the latter should be your second choice.

- **It is people <u>first</u>** before the phone. People come before technology. Turn off the cell phone during church, weddings and funerals. God takes precedence here; nothing else needs to be said.

- **Movie theaters** also need to be free of cell phones beeping. Put your phone on vibrating mode, if necessary. That great line in the movie

---

"It's the way people talk and drive around here."

Here are some tips for safer cell phone use while driving:

- *Use a hands-free system.*

- *Keep conversation short and sweet.*

- *Hang up in tricky traffic situations; safe driving should always take precedence.*

- *Keep more distance between you and the car ahead than normally recommended.*

can totally lose its impact when someone's phone rings at the crucial moment. For example: "Frankly, my dear, I don't give a da - da ding-ding-dom" just wouldn't have the same impact. It can also be irritating to hear a conversation of someone seated next to you.

- **Use cell phones** on the road only during slow traffic. Accidents increase 40% with cell phone usage.

- **Never use the phone in the bathroom** for business. Embarrassment is due if someone on the other end of the phone hears bathroom noises or a toilet flushing. You do deserve some peace, not to mention your listener.

Telephone Tactics

- **Return phone calls** in 24 hours. Some offices say 36 hours is OK, but 24 hours is always the best. If you are going to be out of town, state that in your voice mail message and then make calls back upon your return. If an individual bothers to call you, you should bother to return the call.

- **In an office or business situation, the phone should ring** no more than three times before someone picks it up. If you are calling a residence, letting it ring up to seven times is appropriate. You may have dialed an elderly person, busy parents with small children, or hearing impaired residents who need more time to answer the phone.

- **Smile when you answer that phone.** You are a reflection of your work or family. The voice relays about 50% of the message when you can't see your viewer. Have a tone of pleasantness in your voice. Speak to the person as if you haven't spoken to anyone else all day! (Ha!!!!!) Make them feel special.

- **Identify yourself.** Upon answering the phone, identify yourself even if it's a transferred call. It's amazing the reception you receive when you say, "Hello. This is Luann Alemao and I was inquiring about tickets for the play." It builds a personal connection, not just a telephone voice.

- **When you leave a message or voice mail,** remember to leave your number. It saves that person time from looking it up again in the directory.

- **When taking a message,** ask how to spell the person's name if it is difficult and repeat the spelling back if necessary. That creates the personal touch.

- **Remember to ask for an extension number** and also an appropriate time to return the call. Be aware of time zones when returning calls.

- **If your office is at home** and children are answering the phone, begin to teach them that the telephone is not a toy. If they can't answer the phone properly, they are not ready for that responsibility. The caller doesn't want to play guessing games on the phone with "Who is it?" or have the children shout in their ear, "DAD, It's for YOU!!"

- **To be more effective with the telephone,** leave a message and let the party know when you will be available at home or in your office For example: "John, I will be around from 1-3 p.m. in my office. Call me then." Make sure you're committed to keeping your schedule so you are there to connect with your friends or clients.

- **Be brief, concise and quick.** When leaving a voice mail message, it shouldn't be more than 30 seconds long. If it needs to be longer, ask the person to call you back so you can talk.

Marvelous Message Taking

- Write the person's name and ask for correct spelling of the individual.

- Write time and date of call.

- Write extension number, if applicable.

- Include time zone and an appropriate time to return the call.

- Write the message body and main content of the message.

- Write a telephone number to return the call.

- **Keep away from the cutesy messages** on answering machines. A professional person even with a home office should have a professional sounding voice message. It is not the time or place to have musical tunes or for someone to chant "Nobody's home, nobody's home."

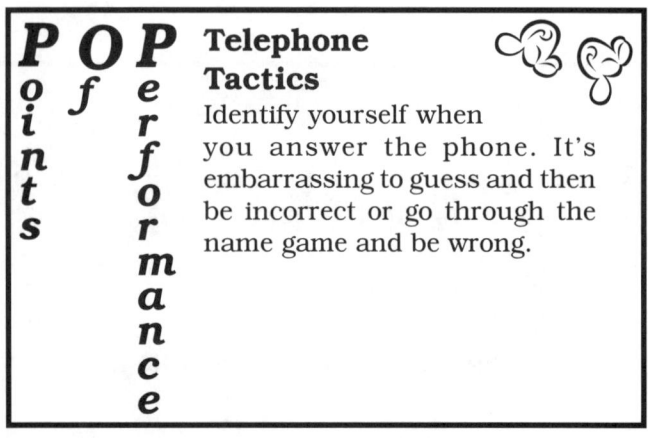

POPf Points of Performance

Telephone Tactics
Identify yourself when you answer the phone. It's embarrassing to guess and then be incorrect or go through the name game and be wrong.

Chapter 5

When and How to Use Business Cards

"It's the handshake left behind."
Maria Everding, Etiquette Institute

Business cards are the best tool anyone could have in business. The business card is the subtle way of saying "I'm here to serve you when you need me." I'm from the school that says educators and all people in business definitely need business cards. The calling card used by the people in the Victorian era is not obsolete; anyone can and should use a business card.

Business Cards

"You can get everything you want in life if you just help enough people get what they want."
Zig Zigler

- **Never leave home without business cards.** It's the best tool you have to create the memory and the retention of you and your business. It's a value-added resource.

- **Present the side of the card with the information** facing the individual you are handing it to. This offers a much more personal touch.

- **Ask questions regarding someone's card.** Questions show a relationship is being built by wanting to know more about the potential customer or acquaintance. It shows you are willing to go the extra mile. Ex: How long have you worked for them? Tell me more about your career. What is your company involved in?

- **At a business meal,** always wait until after the food is ordered before introducing your card. The conversation should be light and airy prior to that.

- **Keep your cards** in a quality container. Digging your card out of a wallet or from the bottom of the handbag can lead to rumpled or bent cards. Neither is a sign of a favorable first impression.

- **Never substitute cards** and give the client an old card or your "other" business card. The correct card should be given out for the precise need. You may forget what service or product was really needed. It's tacky to give out your car sales card when your client really wants insurance.

- **Attach your business card** to every piece of information that leaves your office. You always want to keep your name in front of potential customers. A business card is a great sales tool that you can always refer to. They will never forget you. You can attach your card to brochures, articles you have clipped out, recipes or gifts.

- **It's a personal exchange between one or two people.** Refrain from passing out cards as though you are playing a poker hand. Business card exchange is meant to establish the beginning of a relationship. It loses its effectiveness if you're just out collecting or distributing without merit.

- **Include your business card** in thank you notes that you write. Place the card inside. It is a subtle way of saying, "I can help you when the need arises" instead of stating it as a favor in the thank you note.

- **When including a personal message** on a business card (such as a home phone or some personal information), just draw a line through the business info on the card and include your message on it. You can place a personal message of "Congratulations" or "Blessings on your new office" on the card and just cross out other information.

Chapter 6

Jetiquette
Trains, Planes and Automobiles

In this century, more travel will take place than ever before, so civility is more important than ever before. We share spaces and places more than in the past. Many a new business acquaintance or new relationship has happened in the mode of travel. You'd better be on your best behavior!

Jetiquette-or-Trains, Planes and Automobiles

- **Plan your meetings, vacations and events** to to allow time for delay. (It's almost inevitable.)

- **Drink lots of liquids on long flights**. Flying robs you of bodily fluids and you need to replenish with water or juices, not sodas, coffee or alcohol.

- **Be flexible.** Let colleagues or families sit together. It could be you who needs to stay close to your spouse and two-year-old. Be considerate.

- **Say please and thank you** when served or when special items are brought to your seat. In my survey of flight attendants, their biggest complaint is not hearing the little words "please" and "thank you."

- **Stay out of aisles** when people are boarding. Try to arrange your belongings so you are not standing in the aisle indefinitely. Consider others.

- **Stand up** to let those sitting in the window seat get past you. It's easier than having them crawl or shimmy to the seat. A larger-framed person would appreciate it immensely rather than having to leap frog over you and others.

- **When flying stand-by,** make sure to tell flight attendants. Don't be presumptuous enough to just take a seat. Flight attendants need to be aware of your status to make it easier on other passengers.

- **Be sparing with your carry-on luggage.** The days of golf clubs, hat boxes, shopping bags and the case of wine as carry-ons for one person are over. Be simple so you don't jam up the aisles.

- **Send polite signals** to your seat partner if you don't wish to engage in conversation. For example you can pull out a book, newspaper, or your lap top.

- **Consider the airline club lounge** for rest and layovers. It's secluded and comfortable. It will allow you to work or relax away from heavily trafficed boarding areas.

Auto Travel

- **In the car,** smile and greet everyone with a 'good morning' or 'how was your day'? It doesn't matter if you're car pooling or picking someone up, it's the pleasantry that matters.

- **Smoking** in someone else's car, even if the driver smokes, may not be very well received. The space is small and a little bit of smoke can go a long way.

- **Make the conversation pleasant.** This is not time for off-color remarks or griping about the boss or co-workers. That information needs to be discussed at work. You want your fellow passengers to be glad you are with them, not glad to see you go!

- **Last person out shuts the car door!** Remember to think of others. We shouldn't be in such a big hurry that in pouring down rain or a snow storm we leave the door open so someone else has the inconvenience of getting out to close the door!

- **When you car pool, make sure** the first people to board go to the back of the vehicle so everyone else doesn't have to climb Mt. Everest to find their seat.

Train Travel

- **Make sure you have your train ticket handy** for the attendant to view.

- **Be prepared to meet others** on the train during dinner and snack. It makes the trip much more enjoyable, according to my parents who often travel by train.

- **Try to be respectable** of those sleeping aboard the train.

- **Remember to be organized** with boarding and unboarding because the train won't wait!

Chapter 6 - Jetiquette - Trains, Planes and Automobiles

Tips for the Traveler

- *Make a written list and cross off as you pack the suitcase*

- *Put heavy items such as books, binders and shoes at the bottom of the suitcase.*

- *Slip socks and hosiery into shoes to take up less space.*

- *If you pack expensive jewelry, plan on wearing it. Leaving valuables in a hotel room is not the safest choice.*

- *Don't invite strangers or acquaintances to your room. Arrange to meet them in a highly public place such as the lobby or restaurant.*

- *Have plenty of one dollar bills ready for tipping, cab fares, etc. Keep them in an outside pocket of your pants or handbag, so they are always accessible.*

- *Make sure your contacts and family members know your itinerary and have a phone number.*

- *Plan on carrying your own luggage. It would be naive of you to think that men should assume that role.*

- *Use the corporate travel agent rather than your own personal agency. The corporate agency is usually familiar with travel patterns and amenities that the company is familiar with.*

Grip, Grin & Greet

Points of Performance

Allow everyone to clear the loaded elevator First before you and your party enter. This courtesy will apply in hotels, business buildings and everywhere you travel. People will need to vacate before others can board so what's the use of bottlenecking the door.

If you accidentally push against someone in an elevator say "I'm sorry" or "Please excuse me" quickly and sincerely.

With escalators remember to stand in single file so those in a greater hurry may pass.

Chapter 7

Manners at Play

Public performance and athletic events are the true centers of our communities. Open to all, exclusive of none, these events are places where we can come together with our friends, and share a celebration of human passion, creativity and discipline.
Steve Carignan,
Executive Director, Gallagher-Bluedorn Performing Arts Center

Manners at Play are just as important as in any other environment. You represent yourself and your company when you attend social events. You want to represent your company well. When you attend events such as these you may feel more at ease if you know what is expected of you.

Fine Arts Finesse

"The arts enrich our communities, providing entertainment options for all our residents, and we want new patrons to always feel welcome and comfortable in our performance halls, theaters and exhibit spaces."
Maestro, Jason Weinberger, Music Director and Conductor of the Waterloo/Cedar Falls Symphony

- **Arrive on time.** Artists are live on stage. It is a major faux pas to interrupt the act or movement with tardiness.

- **Keep your cell phone quiet.** Turn it off. Better yet, leave it at home.

- **Applause is a way of thanking the artist.** Applauding is appropriate after each act in a play or after a movement is presented in a concert. A good indication of when the movement of the piece is completed is when the conductor has lowered his/her hands and may even face the audience. When the concert maestro walks on stage and bows, is also a great time to show your appreciation.

- **The usher will lead you to your seats** in a theater or auditorium. The female follows the usher to the seats and the male follows behind.

- **Exit only** after a complete number or between acts. Exit quietly and immediately if you are having a fit of coughing or a child is crying or has an emergency.

- **Love birds,** be considerate of your audience. This is an instance where two heads together is not better than one.

- **Thou shalt not talk,** hum or sing along unless the audience has been requested to participate. Keeping time with a body part is rude and distracting.

- **Go easy on the "Old Spice."** Many people are allergic to heavy scents and perfumes.

Patriotism

- **Citizens should be in the habit of removing their hats as respect for the flag.** Whether you're at a sporting event, military funeral or social event, the hat should be removed. If the flag is passing by in a parade, stand and show reverence for the flag and for our country. Some exceptions for women are: At a social event the hat may remain on.

- **Place your right hand over your heart and remove your hat when saying the Pledge of Allegiance.** Stand and try to recite the words with the crowd if you can.

- **Keep gum, drinks, food and other distractions silent** during the playing of the national anthem. This is a time of respect and reverence.

At the Movies

So what is proper behavior at the movies? When is the last time you wanted to squelch that person's slurping of their drink or answer your neighbors cell phone and say "They're busy!". What about the knees of the person behind you that have been rubbing your back all evening because they are keeping time with the musical score? Have respect for those around you. Here is a short refresher course on movie manners.

- **Limit the talking**. People behind and around you don't want to hear you relaying the next scene of the movie. Let all attending be surprised. Be considerate of other people. They paid for their ticket as well.

- **Be Punctual.** If you find yourself running behind take your seats quickly. This is not the time to stand in the aisle and report that sitting in the first few rows makes you dizzy. Check your local newspaper for the proper time. Most theater ads allow for some tardiness.

- **The Snacks.** Eating at the movies is one of the pleasures. Remember to chew with your mouth closed and resist chewing gum if you have an urge to pop or smack. Carry out your own trash. If you bring it in, take it out with you.

- **Should we take the children?** If there is doubt they might be frightened or their attention span is short, take them to a kids movie where the rules aren't so rigid and people expect kids in the aisles to use the restroom or concession stand.

- **Howling Hormones.** Save the body movements for a more private time and place.

- **Gross Grooming.** Theater managers have actually found fingernail and toenails clippings on the floor of theaters. Grooming belongs at home.

The Sport of It

"Always let the "Game" be a Game and not any more."
Tony Dicecco, Women's Basketball Coach
University of Northern Iowa

Many times our business turns into play whether we're a participant or a spectator. We want to be role models for the new employees and our own children. A local coach in my community passes out these reminders to parents and athletes every year:

- **Follow the rules.** Every competition has its own set of rules. A person who doesn't follow the rules probably won't be asked to join in next time.

- **Greet everyone** with a handshake and a smile.

- **Make sure you know the proper attire for the event.** If it's a private club there may be some restrictions. If it's a court or track, certain style shoes may need to be worn.

- **Keep rejoicing in check!** Never brag about your ability or pretend your level of play exceeds others. Let your partners discover for themselves the ability that you have.

- **Watch your language.** Profanity is never appropriate and will ruin your integrity. Your company name is represented in your decorum and language.

- **Don't argue about the rules or the call.** Just play or observe the game.

- **Your voice level should depend on the event.** Having fun and laughing is one thing, but belly laughter and loudmouth joking may become annoying. Events such as a tennis match, golf or fishing require a sense of self-control and decorum.

- **Be on Time.** In sporting events such as golf, a tee time is important to maintain promptness. You don't want your golf partners waiting for you so they can "tee off."

Chapter 8

Manners for Many Occasions

As life happens, we encounter many scenarios where finesse can ease us through, so you don't have to look like a moron.

We have the skills to make others feel comfortable and view us as kind and caring people. Manners are learned and not earned and the situations of life can test our ability to handle them appropriately and courteously.

Compliments

"The measure of a truly great man is the courtesy with which he treats lesser men."

- **Be gracious** when you receive a compliment. Say "Thank you, that was nice," "I appreciate your kind words," etc. Make the sender feel good for relaying a compliment.

- **Avoid making the person who compliments you feel awkward.** For example: If someone compliments you on your dress or suit he/she may feel awkward if you respond, "This old thing; I've had it for years."

- **Give credit when credit is due.** Give credit from the bottom to the top. The effective leader makes sure to compliment the janitorial staff as well as the organizer or chairman of the project.

- **Be kind and sincere.** Sincere praise and thanks is better than anything else. Try to find something kind and sincere whether it's a job performance evaluation, a project completed, or a new article of clothing. Genuine comments are the best reward.

Speech

"The best way to persuade others is with our ears."
Rusk

- **Listen twice as much as you speak.** You'll be noted as the great conversationalist.

- **Don't finish someone's sentence.** You'll come across as impatient and a little possessive, instead of helpful.

- **Let everyone speak once before you speak twice.** This is a great rule when meeting new or unfamiliar people.

- **Be aware of your verbal fillers.** Examples are like, um, er, ya know, whatever, etc. Get the idea? ANNOYING!

- **Say "Yes" vs. "Yeah."** "Yes" is used in conversation. "Yeah" is informal and should be avoided at formal business events.

- **Pausing in speech** is permissible to gather your thoughts.

- **Watch your sexist comments** such as: "you guys." Refer to a mixed group as ladies and gentlemen, or people. "You folks" is permissible in some parts of the country.

- **"No problem" is one of the biggest speech faux pas.** You are insinuating that the customer or the incident was a problem. How about saying, "You're welcome!" It's never gone out of style.

Tips for (Speech) Tics

- **Use pauses more often in your speech,** instead of um, er, like and you know.

- **Use phrases such as** "Let me get my thoughts together" or "Let me think about this" before you speak, so you don't start off saying "UMMM........."

- **Join your local Toastmasters International Club** if you're serious about honing your speaking skills.

- **Tape yourself** and let your ears hear the speech tics. You will be amazed!

- **Watch video movies** of yourself. Listen and be cognizant of your speech.

Conversation Starters and Stoppers

"Do not wait for leaders, do it person to person."
Mother Teresa

- **Use open-ended questions** (tell me why, etc.). Questions such as "How do you know the hosts? Where are you from? The food is superb. What have you tried? Have you tried the artichoke dip? will lead to more conversation rather than, "Nice party, huh?"

- **Ask questions** to get to know people. Don't just talk about yourself. "Where would you locate the new library?" "I heard you've been to Portugal. What is it like?"

- **Stay away from topics** such as politics and religion. These topics are open to confrontation and combativeness. They are taboo in many cultures.

- **Use grammatically correct words.** For example "Yes" not "Yeah," or "Did you eat?" not "Jeat?" etc.

- **Be careful** using oxymorons (pretty ugly, awfully good).

- **In a group,** let everyone speak once before you speak twice.

- **No one** has ever listened themselves out of a job. You have heard God gave us two ears and only one mouth so twice as much listening could occur as speaking.

- **Children should learn not to interrupt adults,** unless it's an emergency. Children saying, "Excuse me" should not give them permission to interrupt. Let them know what constitutes an emergency: someone is hurt or about to be hurt, or a toddler needs to use the bathroom NOW.

- **Teach children a silent signal** when they can speak so as not to disrupt conversation. Children can approach Mom and Dad and stand very close or make eye contact with them to let them know they need to speak.

Remembering Names

"The mind is a wonderful thing, but why does it leave me when I have to remember a name?"
Luann Alemao

- **Use names frequently in conversation with the individual.** The more you call someone by name, the more you'll remember it.

- **Ask people to spell their name** for you. I use this strategy when it's an unusual name or when I didn't fully hear it. It shows a personal interest.

- **Admit it if you don't remember a name; you're not a walking phone directory.** You can say, "Refresh my memory; I don't remember your name" rather than "What's your name again? It was unusual and I want to remember it."

- **Use association or other strategies to remember names.** Picture the person and some association. You might try, "Harry is hairy" or someone else with the same name that sometimes helps you make the association.

- **Remember to write down the name as you are speaking to someone on the phone** so you can use the name in conversation. Always have a pad of paper by the phone for jotting down names of people you speak to.

Sympathy Etiquette

"People don't care how much you know, until they know how much you care."
Cavett Robert, National Speakers Association

- **Just say "I'm so sorry"** when you encounter a member of the family who has lost a loved one. That is all that's needed be said.

- **You could relay to the family a special moment** or kindness the deceased was involved in with you. For example: talk about how Sam always came through with the project; Sarah always remembered your birthday, etc.

- **Refrain from saying** "It's God's will" or "God doesn't give us anything we can't bear." Right now *it is* too hard to bear.

- **Remember to include individuals** in functions after their loved one's death. It is important they are still included in the company or festivity such as the annual picnic, Christmas party and after hours socializing. That's when they need the human interaction the most.

- **Be comfortable when they bring up their loved one.** They still have memories, a history and feelings for their loved one.

- **Send a condolence or sympathy card.** Some people express themselves better in writing. You are letting the bereaved know that you are in thought and prayer.

Chapter 9

Office Manners

It takes everyone working together in the office to meet all the demands that take place everyday. Much has changed in the work environment—longevity, increasing technology, loss of loyalty. One thing that hasn't changed is people doing business with people. Building effective relationships with our colleagues and clients is still of the utmost importance. People want to do business with courtesy and trust. The relationships you build in the office and outside the office will be to your advantage in the future.

Networking

"When you talk you only hear what you already know."

To maximize the experience of networking, here are some tips. These tips are winning ways with networking and will start you on the value-added conversation path. I always want to keep in mind that you want people to be glad you entered the room, not happier because you left.

- **Remember the 10 foot rule.** Acknowledge anyone that is within 10 feet of you. If you're in the office place, on the street, or in the mall, a simple "Hello" can add verbal sunshine to anyone's day. One of the biggest complaints of corporate America is that people don't even say a "Hello" or "Goodbye" to fellow co-workers.

- **Wear your name tag** on the right side.

- **Hold your drink** in the left hand. You never want to offer a cold, wet hand to shake or wipe it off on your skirt or pants before you greet someone.

- **Smile;** it's the language understood around the globe.

- **Find someone** you would like to meet and go meet them. Have some idea who will be attending and who you would like to meet. At a function where you don't know anyone, spending 5-7 minutes with a group is sufficient before you move on.

Chapter 9 - Office Manners

- **Never think gender specific**. Think professional. For example, don't think that the president or CEO isn't the woman standing over in the corner sipping on her drink. Stereotyping doesn't belong in the work place.

- **When you encounter** a group of people conversing, introduce yourself when there is a pause in the conversation.

- **Bring your business cards** in a holder. It makes much more of an impression to pull cards out of a nice holder than digging to the bottom of the handbag or searching in a wallet and pulling out a bent, dog eared card.

- **Prepare a 15-second commercial** about yourself and your business. You will be remembered much more readily.

- **Be prepared.** Know who will be there and the format of the event. Seek out those who can develop your business. Don't wait for them to come to you.

- **Be discrete** in handing out your card. It should be a personal exchange between one to two people. It's not a poker game with the ante increasing.

- **Follow up.** Keep the promises you made. Remember to send that article that you promised, write a note, or give them a call.

**"Good Office Manners
Equals Professionalism"**

Points Of Performance

Attending Business Meetings:

Be prompt. Stick to the meeting agenda. Pour your water or soft drink in a glass rather than drinking from the can. If running an effective meeting is crucial to your position, join Toastmasters International. They have many strategies and workbooks that offer help and advice in for the meeting platform. You would rather people say "that meeting went quickly and we really worked" than "I couldn't stop looking at my watch. Everyone went on tangents and we didn't accomplish what we needed to."

Points Of Performance

Praise Loudly

If you must reprimand an employee do so in private. Keep the embarrassment to a minimum. Find them doing something right later and make sure you praise them sincerely.

The Bully

"Nothing is so strong as gentleness, nothing so gentle as strength."
St. Francis

- **Bullies are someone you may have to face** at work, school, or dealing with the public. Refrain from getting into an argument with the bully. Just leave. You won't win and their goal is the surrender and the embarrassment of making you give in to them.

- **What they say or the way they behave** is a reflection of them, not you. They usually have a difficult time with friendships.

- **When bullies put the pressure on,** resist. Simply say "no." If they become forceful, tell an adult or supervisor. In the office situation, clients have shared with me that other co-workers might demand that a project be done a certain style or format. These bullies love to issue orders that they do not have jurisdiction for.

Pregnancy Protocol

- **Do make sure your supervisor** is among the first to know the news and doesn't learn it from co-workers. It also gives you a chance to let him/her know your plans for returning to work. If a sick day is needed, supervisors will be more flexible if you have prepared them.

- **Keep your sense of humor.** Some individuals just use poor judgment by making sexual or snide comments regarding pregnancy. "YOU'RE PREGNANT AGAIN!" "WAS THIS ONE PLANNED?" are just some of the comments that roll off people's tongues. Be prepared!

- **If a colleague is pregnant, wish her well,** and continue with the business at hand. Many women feel more comfortable discussing work than their condition.

- **This is not an invitation to touch bellies!** Many people feel pregnancy is an invitation to touch when they never even offered a hug or an arm before.

Office Party

Even with tight budget constraints, people generally love the office party. In cost-cutting, downsizing economies, corporations are spending top dollar for company holiday parties. According to career counselors, the office party is still featured as a top event. But if you're ready to just put your feet up, turn in and skip the festivity, that's pretty risky, say career counselors around the nation.

Here are some tips to enhance that office party:

- **It may be a *party*,** but it's still important for you to attend. Your boss may look over the name tags that are left over. Absences are missed. Why would a boss be irritated? What if you spent hundreds of dollars on food and drink and only a few employees show up?

- **This is a chance to network** and build some additional relationships. Your co-workers will have a chance to be better acquainted with you as well.

- **Watch your consumption of alcohol.** It is still a work setting where your behavior should be in check.

- **If you really detest going** and can't bear the small talk, stop in for a brief time.

- **DON'T GOSSIP.** You don't know who came with whom or what spouse is standing in ear shot of your conversation.

- **Watch your physical behavior.** This is not time to make out or hit on your spouse, date, or significant other.

- **Don't let cupid get stupid.** This is also not the time to make a pass or hit on a fellow co-worker. In most corporations that is considered inappropriate or brazen behavior.

Be Social and Suave

Business after Hours, tailgates are just a small sample of the events you may be asked to attend in the workplace. A major corporate function can enhance your career or ruin it. Having the confidence of what to wear and what behavior is expected may put some of those butterflies to rest.

Cocktail Party :
also known as
"Business After Hours" Celebrating
usually consists of hors d'oeuvres and is immediately following business working hours 5-7 p.m.
Guests will stand and business attire is expected

Cocktail and buffet
drinks and dinner foods
2-4 hours between 6-9 p.m.
guests will seat themselves and sit at random tables
Business attire is preferred

Brunch
combination of breakfast and lunch foods,
dessert items occasionally
may be seat down or a buffet
may have reserved seating
served between 10-2 p.m.
business casual or professional business attire

Dinner
seat down meal may include several courses
usually between 6-9 p.m.
Hint: the more courses served the more formal the restaurant
business casual - formal business attire depending on formality of restaurant

Picnic
Held: outdoors
Food: casual foods such as burgers, brats, sandwiches,
using fingers, paper and plastic utensils
Time: 12 noon-5:00 pm
Dress: Casual (if a business function, jeans may not be appropriate)

Tailgate Party
Held: outside in a sporting arena parking lot or before a concert event held in a covered tent or the back of a pickup or car bed
Foods: usually finger foods, burgers, chicken, vegetables, fruit kabobs, etc. and tailgate used as a serving table
Time: usually 2 hours before the event is scheduled.
Dress: Casual Attire

Pool or Beach Party
Held: around a private or club pool or beach
Food: variety of food, such as finger foods, gourmet items, grilled meats, etc.
Dress: If wearing a swimming suit an appropriate cover-up is necessary
Bring an extra change of casual business clothing
Time: Afternoon or Evening Swim

Party Queues

- *Don't overdress unless invitations state formal or casual dress. Find out as much as you can about the function. Knowing who will be there will make it more relaxing for you.*

- *Women can wear a dressy holiday outfit, pants, skirt, or dress for the more formal affair. A dressy business suit would be quite appropriate as well. Solid colors work nicely for holiday attire. Just add some sparkly earrings and a necklace.*

- *The sequins and glitz may be a mistake. Consult with colleagues beforehand to see what was worn in previous years.*

- *Refrain from your tightest, shortest or the most revealing. Dressing professionally for any of these social business occasions is very important.*

- *Remember to acknowledge the supervisor, chairman, president and spouses. You wouldn't want to snub the guest of honor at any function.*

What to Wear to the Party

- **Don't overdress** unless invitations state formal or casual dress.

- **Women can wear** a dressy holiday outfit, pants, skirt, or dress. A dressy business suit would be quite appropriate as well. Solid colors work nicely for holiday attire. Just add some sparkly earrings and a necklace.

- **The sequins and glitz** may be a mistake. Consult with colleagues beforehand to see what was worn in previous years.

Chapter 10

Dress for the Interview

Can a bad first impression keep you from getting the job? According to NACE, (National Association of Colleges and Employers), the answer is yes. An overall general appearance does cause an employer to pause and evaluate. If you are a seasoned professional, it might be enough for the supervisor to comment on clothing that he/she feels is inappropriate for the job. A client shared with me that his supervisor was pretty agitated when he showed up for work in shorts. He genuinely thought he was professional. It was during hot weather and he wanted to be comfortable.

What should be included in a job interview wardrobe for women and men?

- Modest length skirt (2 inches above the knee is usually safe or longer).

- Stay away from body piercing.

- Stocking or socks that are an extension of the hem line. First of all, make sure you wear them!

- If you are wearing pants that have belt loops, wear a belt. No exceptions.

- Double-breasted jackets are to remain buttoned at all times.

- Make sure to shake hands. It may have more impact than you realize.

- Hairstyles should be neatly coifed. This is not time to try something new.

- Keep gum in your pocket or handbag. Entering an interview chewing is a sure way to eliminate yourself from the running, immediately.

- Keep a spare pair of nylons on hand.

- To be safe, beard and mustaches should be avoided until after you have been hired.

- Clothes should be pressed and clean.

- No obvious tattoos.

Chapter 10 - Dress for the Interview

***P**oints* ***O**f* ***P**erformance*

Have a Jacket

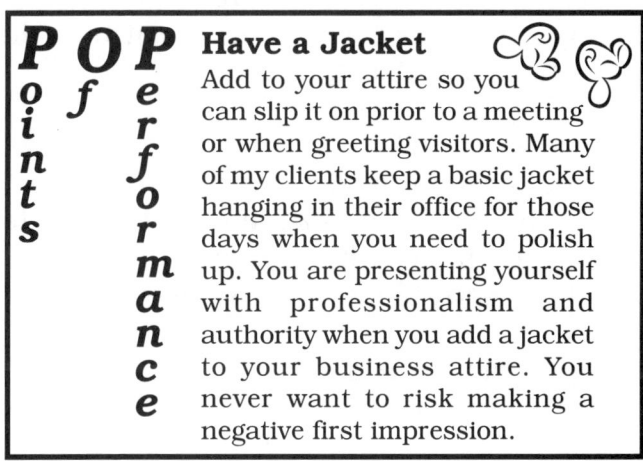

Add to your attire so you can slip it on prior to a meeting or when greeting visitors. Many of my clients keep a basic jacket hanging in their office for those days when you need to polish up. You are presenting yourself with professionalism and authority when you add a jacket to your business attire. You never want to risk making a negative first impression.

5 Winning Wardrobe Wonders

"The best accessory a woman can have is a well-dressed man."
Bob Sawyer, Clothier

Males
1 suit (slacks and jacket)
1 navy blazer
1 pair of quality khaki slacks
1 mock neck, or 3-button polo neck silk sweatershirt
1 colored white or oxford blue dress shirt
Quality accessories would be: a leather belt, leather shoes, socks

Females
1 quality jacket (navy, black or tan)
1 ankle-length lined skirt (navy, black, or tan)
1 pair of pants (black, navy or tan)
1 white or ecru blouse - short sleeve and long sleeve
1 colored blouse or shirt
Accessories would include: quality shoes, belt and handbag. Scarves with multiple colors and jewelry

Buy the highest quality you can afford. This is investment dressing. Remember, you are judged from the top down. Your handbag, briefcase and shoes should also be of top quality. Trends may not be any indication of quality.

Thought to remember: Your visual resume may say more than your written one!

Chapter 11

Present Protocol or Gift Glitches

It is more fun to give than receive, is the old cliché. Remembering a friend with a gift is usually easy. The fun is in the selection of the gift. The business gift giving comes with a few more details to keep in mind. Many of my clients want to know if they take part in a clients' or co-workers' personal celebrations or ill fortunes. There is an art to business gift-giving so that we appear gracious, kind and professional.

Present Protocol or Gift Glitches

> *"The most appreciated gift says,*
> *'I thought about you.'"*
> Maria Everding, Etiquette Institute

- **Use discretion** when sending gifts across cultural lines. For example: Leather items are found offensive for the Eastern Indian culture since cows are considered sacred.

- **Presents for the boss** are often considered inappropriate because of the connotation of being a bribe. It's better to go in on a group gift for the boss. Caveat: If you have worked for the boss for an extended period of time, a gift is probably okay. If you are the new kid on the block, the gift can be misconstrued.

- **Use discretion when giving presents to co-workers and staff.** It's a thoughtful gesture to remember a co-worker's birthday, anniversary, or new baby, but when you consider how many gifts that could potentially be, it's a good idea to know gifts aren't always necessary. Often a card or a kind word is just as nice. (I have a standard card gift of a nice bookmark that I include in the card to remember people.)

- **If you are visiting friends** the old rule of a hostess gift still applies. Select a gift of candies or homemade confections. Hosts love something like homemade salsa, or homemade rosemary herb vinegar. Plants would be an alternative, or a good bottle of wine or sparkling beverage.

Chapter 11 - Present Protocol or Gift Glitches

- **Overnight or weekend guest.** Take a gift with you. A gift basket of the food products from the local area is my standby gift. It could be wine, cheese, flavored nuts, or candy made in the local area all collected in an attractive gift basket. I sometimes insert a Christmas ornament from our area so our friends or relatives remember when we came to visit. You can choose to send a gift after you return home and have seen their tastes and what they might want or need.

- **Should the wine or food guests bring be served at the dinner party?** The menu is already planned, so unless it's a potluck supper, the host or hostess will already have the beverages planned. As a guest you can ease the situation with a note or spoken word of "save and enjoy this for another time."

- **Graduation gifts or announcements:** In many communities, open house graduations are in style. You may be invited to 15 or more "open houses." Are you to give the $20-100 average gift to all 15? Remember that graduation announcements do not equal gifts. You are not obligated to give, although you may choose to do so. You should remember the graduate with a congratulatory note. Open houses are more a way of saying "share in my success, you mean a lot to me."

The Last Wrap on Gifts

- **Thank you notes** are a good way to let people know how much you appreciate their thoughtfulness. If you're not sure whether to send one, it's better to error on the polite side.

- **You are excused from sending a thank you** for the hostess gift. That would be saying thank you for the thank you and it's not necessary.

- **Send a written thank you card** for your wedding, shower, birthday, or graduation gifts. E-mail thank yous are only appropriate for the casual lunch someone bought. Be on the polite side and error with graciousness.

Chapter 12

Entertaining 101

Today one of our biggest social commitments is the entertaining that business and personal life requires. In the business of living with events such as graduations, retirements, promotions and births, entertaining takes place. We may want to thank the neighbor for a kind deed, take an existing client out to dine or have family over for a festivity. According to many experts, the future will bring more entertaining close to home.

One of the best <u>and</u> worst places to make a mistake is around the table. How can you obtain that dining finesse? It's like everything else you do, golf, gardening, singing—you practice, practice, practice!

Entertaining 101

"The most important rule of entertaining is to make sure your guests are having a good time."

- **When asked to someone's home for dinner,** remember the hostess gift such as wine, candy, or a homemade confection.

- **Flowers should be sent** before the party and not brought to the party. Vases are never where they should be and your hostess may have to scramble trying to put the flowers into water.

- **Plan ahead** and make some of the selections and freeze them. You will be less hassled when company arrives.

- **Plan an interesting and stimulating chemistry of people**, people who haven't met before, people with similar interests, etc. For smaller dinner parties this is more critical, be prepared, if you plan people who are in total opposition of one another on social, political or civic issues.

- **Have a party** where the preparation is the party. A taco bar where everyone builds their own, an oriental stir fry party where the spouses prepare and make the dinner, assembling your own personal pizzas.

- **Keep the centerpiece low** so conversation has a chance to develop and people can make eye contact with one another. That beautiful arrangement with the tall peacock feathers would look great placed in another location as well.

Toasting

The tradition of toasting began with the ancient Greeks as an act of good faith. The host took the first sip, thus assuring guests that the beverage was not laced with poison, a common occurrence in those days. That is why the most common toast heard globally is "To your health." Later, during the Roman Empire, a small piece of burnt bread, known as "toast," mellowed the flavor of wine being offered which is how the term toast originated.

Guidelines for the Perfect Toast

- Your toast should be rehearsed, but shouldn't sound rehearsed.

- Always stand.

- Use personal anecdotes to liven up the toast.

- Make a toast that is free of profanity.

- You can toast without alcohol. Any beverage will do.

- Avoid chewing gum.

- Watch annoying mannerisms such as jingling keys and coins or tapping your foot.

- If you are the honoree, wait until everyone has sipped from their beverage before you do so, to avoid toasting yourself.

Wine Serving and Selection

"Wine drinking is exploration".
Jim Duarte,
Owner of Duarte Nursery and Vineyards
Hughson, California

- **Questions about wine?** Ask the sommelier (wine steward). At the restaurant, they are the experts and can answer your questions.

- **Don't be intimidated** about wine selection. It's better to have help than choose a wine that is not compatible with your meal. Let the wine steward do his or her job to help you.

- **Bringing the wine to the table.** The wine steward will show you the bottle that you have ordered. He/she will pour some in a glass and ask you to taste. Most people, wine connoisseurs or not, can taste large defects in wine. Yet, most people don't have the self-assurance to reject a wine if it truly is bad. If you find the taste flawed, do say something.

- **Hold the wine glass by the stem.** Most people hold wine by the bowl of the glass and that warms it up. The glass should only be filled two-thirds full to let the wine breathe and let the flavors permeate.

- **Think about your food first, then select the wine.** The old rule of white with white meat and red for more robust entrees still applies with some exceptions.

- **Match the food to the wine**, says Jim Duarte, owner of Duarte Nurseries and Vineyards. Jim says, "The more seasoned the food is, the heavier or more body the wine can be." Balance the spiciness with the proper wine.

- **Think big glasses for red and smaller for white wines.** Red wines particularly need more room to breathe and release their fruity aromas.

- **Watch the temperature.** Red wines are best served around 68 degrees and white wines may be chilled or served from the refrigerator. Over-chilling can kill the taste of the wine.

- **Try the house wine.** It's usually the most affordable. If you find that you like it, probably, the rest of the list will be satisfactory.

Wine and Food

Fish
Simply broiled
A clean, sharp, white wine

Salads
Crisp, lively wine, not to clash with the dressing

Fruit desserts
apricot, peach or plum
Sweet wines with a hint of honey

Cheese
White wine is usually the best

Poultry & Beef
Think red or white
More seasoned the entree, the heavier the wine

Disaster Dilemmas

- **If can't find the toilet paper in another home,** you are free to look for some in the bathroom. For all who have guests over and entertain, make sure extra toilet paper is in an obvious place and guests do not have to hunt. It should be in plain sight.

- **Plumbing problems?** Let your host or hostess know rather discretely. They can take care of it from there. Don't just pass it off as nothing. The party could be even more embarrassing if the plumbing is left unattended.

- **Calling someone by the wrong name.** Just apologize and go on. Don't fall all over yourself with apologies. It can happen to anyone.

- **Spilling on one's dinner partner:** A most sincere apology is in order. Crawling under the table to retrieve lost food or mopping up your guest is inappropriate. Offer your napkin to your guest if it's clean, or put your napkin on the table if the spill is running.

- **XYZ (examine your zipper).** This is an old acronym to indicate that you need to examine your fly. If you see someone with this dilemma, one of the most subtle ways to handle it is to say in a normal conversational tone, "Check your fly," just as if your were saying, *"The report is due on Friday."* This same scenario works well for the person who has broccoli between their front teeth or a tear, hole, unbuttoned garment, or a hosiery run in a precarious place.

Chapter 13

Dining with Delight

- **Place handbags and briefcases** on the floor by the left of your chair. Refrain from slinging them on the back of the chair or using a vacant chair.

- **Gentlemen should remove their hats** and put them on a coat hook or on an unoccupied chair. This means sporting caps, seed caps, hunting hats, etc. All should remain off while eating. The caveat is at an informal picnic or outside in the sun. While eating, in this circumstance hats are permissible.

- **When refusing a beverage,** wine, coffee etc., just tell the waiter "No, thank you" or make a gesture over the glass that you do not care for any. It is not necessary to turn the glass over or place it elsewhere on the table.

- **Refrain from** picking your teeth, applying makeup at the table, or combing your hair. Excuse yourself and visit the restroom.

- **Work from the outside** in with the silverware. Start with the spoon or the fork that is furthest away as each course is served. The other hint is to watch someone else who has more finesse than you do!

- **Glasses** belong on the right.

- **Plates, salad, or dessert** if brought before you have completed your meal are placed on the left.

- **If you must excuse yourself** to use the phone or restroom, place your napkin on the table to the left side of your plate, not on the chair.

- **For men,** your tie should stay hanging from your neck, not flipped over your shoulder while dining.

- **Napkins** belong on your lap when you sit down. Fold one corner down into triangle on your lap and you will not have to worry about it falling on the floor.

- **Blessings or Grace** at someone else's home can be awkward. We bow our head in reverence to the words that are spoken in any language or religion.

- **When dining at someone's home,** make sure you take a small sampling of all dishes that are passed around. In some cultures, it is extremely rude not to taste or sample all food served.

- **Only read** at the table when you are alone. It's rude to have your head in a book when people are seated at the table with you. At work, find a place outdoors to read or go back to your office rather than reading at the break room table.

- **Keep conversation** away from politics and religion. Use open-ended questions that will prompt discussion. If entertaining global guests, this suggestion is even more crucial.

- **When dining at a buffet**, don't park yourself at the buffet line. Get what you want to eat and circulate.

Tips on Tipping

- **Tipping** is an indication of the service received, not the food. If you didn't care for the food selection, that is not a part of the service.

- **When service is not satisfactory**, avoid leaving just pennies or dimes. Leave a smaller percentage such as 5 or 8% of the bill. The best advice you could leave is to let a supervisor know about the dissatisfaction so improvement can be made.

- **If you're dining with a group and no one seems to be leaving the tip**, volunteer to do so. You don't want the reputation of being cheap on your conscience. It's a reflection of you and who you represent.

- **If the food is not sufficient**, just remark how great the service was and leave some additional money.

- **The standard tip is at least 15% of the total charges**. In addition, there may be others who you should tip such as the wine steward, the coat check attendant, or the parking valet.

How Do We Eat It?

Corn on the cob with fingers or holders.

French Fries (picnic) with fingers.

French Fries (fine dining restaurant) with utensils, cut with fork and then dip in ketchup.

Asparagus may be eaten with fingers unless covered with sauce or too limp to eat without making an extreme mess. It is always permissible to eat with a knife and fork.

Strawberries, grapes, cherries with stem remaining can be picked up with fingers and eaten with fingers; discretely remove pits or seeds from your mouth with fingers.

Strawberries, grapes, dipped in chocolate, sauce or sugared are eaten with fingers and may be placed in a frill. Remember to pick the paper frill up as well and leave the paper frill on your plate after consuming the food inside.

Fruit served on plate, melon slices, kiwi, strawberries, etc. knife and fork are used.

Fried Chicken (in restaurant or in someone's home) Use your knife and fork. Eat only the meat you can retrieve with your knife and fork. Leave what you can't successfully remove with utensils.

Chicken (picnic or fast food) Use those fingers and refrain from licking your fingers; use your napkin especially if it's a business social event. Behind closed doors with the curtains pulled you may use your fingers.

Dry Crisp Bacon may be eaten with fingers.

Artichokes pull the leaf off the plant, dip it in sauce, and using your top teeth, scrape the meat off the leaf and discard the leaf on plate. Use your knife and fork to eat the "heart" and base.

Avocados if served by the half eat with a spoon. If served in a salad, use your fork.

Baked Potato squeeze whole potato together and cut to add butter, sour cream, etc. You may eat the peeling of your potato and leave the foil surrounding the potato on your plate.

Pasta eat only a few strands or pieces at a time. Twirl the fork if long strands are served such as linguini, angel hair, etc. Do not use a spoon.

Sandwiches most sandwiches are made to be eaten with the hands. If the sandwich is messy, too tall to fit in the mouth, or just oozing with gooey fillings, use your knife and fork. Use your knife to cut any sandwich so you can manipulate it easier.

Olives, pickles, deviled eggs, chips, Finger foods, but generally will not be served at formal dinner affairs.

Fish may be served with fish fork which is smaller than salad fork to remove small pieces. It will probably be served with a knife and fork.

Chapter 13 - Dining with Delight

Hint :
Avoid difficult foods when dining with business associates or people you are being acquainted with for the first time.

Terms on the Menu

antipasto	first course, usually served cold
au gratin	a topping of browned bread crumbs or cheese
au jour	"of the day," The specialty of the house
bisque	a rich cream soup, usually containing fish or shellfish
bernaise	a sauce with tarragon
boeuf	beef
bouillabaisse	fish chowder
brioche	A French yeast roll, rich in butter. A topknot is characteristic of this roll
café glacé	coffee ice cream
canapé	small open -faced sandwich
citron	lemon

coq au vin	chicken in wine sauce
creme	cream
demitasse	strong black coffee
café au lait	coffee with milk
Florentine	with spinach
hors d'oeuvres	appetizers
legumes	peas or beans
Mornay	white cheese sauce
mousse	light dessert of cream and eggs
parfait	frozen, ice cream or custard dessert layered in a tall narrow glass
pesto	sauce heavy in basil and garlic, mixed with olive oil
petit	small
potage	soup with cream base
poulet	chicken
primavera	pasta with "spring" fresh vegetables in a sauce
quiche	a tart of eggs and cheese in a crust or pastry

ratatouille	mixed vegetables, generally containing eggplant
sorbet	fruit sherbet, may be served as a palette cleanser
souffle	puffed dish with eggs, cheese, etc.
sauté	to cook in a small amount of oil or fat
tarimasu	a dessert made of layered lady fingers, creme, fruit and liqueurs
Vichyssoise	cold potato soup
vinagrette	salad dressing

Chapter 14

Hospitality

Hospitality is the key to solid business relationships and lasting friendship. Where I live, the travel and tourism board use a slogan of "Come be our guest." They feel that hospitality is the name of their game. If one patron in business doesn't live up to that slogan, they have told an untruth and customer service, tourism and hospitality have suffered greatly.

In our society, civility is also the name of the game. It's how we pick and select friends, choose an organization, even a pre-school for our children. How we are treated is basic in our society. The ability to make people feel at home, to make them feel #1, is a real gift.

When growing up, hospitality was just part of our lifestyle. We entertained constantly and were brought up to be gracious, and to greet people by name and just roll out the red carpet.

When people are treated with respect, they look beyond the moment, they behave with civility. Likewise, when children are taught manners, they are pleasant individuals.

Some Hit Party Ideas and Menus

Entertaining at home is making a comeback! Here are some ideas that will create a hit with family, friends, and co-workers. They are simple ideas. You don't need months to plan and you'll have memories to last a lifetime. Most of these ideas can be used at the office or for entertaining at home for friends and family.

All of these events are ones I've either planned or enjoyed. They were a hit and just loads of fun. They are well-chewed and promise some real laughter, blessings and many memories.

The Cookie Exchange

This started in our neighborhood about 20 years ago and is a great way to get to know the neighbors or the gals at work.

Have everyone bring 2 to 3 dozen cookies packaged in 1/2 dozen packages. Ask everyone to also bring about 1/2 dozen cookies to sample from their home cookie jar at home, the bakery, their own kitchen, etc. No one should be excluded if they don't have time to bake or don't like to.

The amount brought to exchange is the amount the person takes home. You leave with as much as you brought. What an array of cookies and candies you'll receive this way!

We arrange the cookie packages on a table and everyone forms a line and selects once before anyone selects twice. Many times the recipe is included in the packaged cookies. Continue around the table until all the packaged cookies have owners. Put on the coffee pot to perk. Serve hot cider and you have a great fellowship opportunity.

Trim the Tree

This entertaining idea is rich in friendship and love. It can be done by young and old, single and married. It's another great way to include that new neighbor or neighbors who moved in down the street or someone that can't make it home for the holidays.

This tradition was started by our dear friends who have traveled with this idea to Guam, New York, Michigan, South Dakota, Nebraska and Iowa. What a lively, fun way to get your tree decorated. They started it in their single days and have continued it for 30 plus years.

Trim the Tree can also be a time for guests to help in making some of the tree decorations. The guests would hang decorations on the tree after they're made. Each year a new ornament can be made. Instructions are available on a table laid out with all the supplies for the annual ornament. Children, parents and grandparents take part in making the ornaments

The ornaments in years past have included origami, paper chains for the little ones to make, stringing cranberries, etc. Many ornaments from previous years are hung on the tree as boxes are unpacked from years past.

We can share about ourselves and learn so much about our friends as we unpack the ornaments we've gathered. After making ornaments and trimming the tree, it's chili time with all the fixin's. The menu consists of chili, fresh vegetables and all the holiday confections you could muster. We also have a table of appetizers to munch on as we are decorating and conversing.

We end the evening singing Christmas carols. The musical guests may play solos or duets with instruments. Together we are gathered around that freshly cut pine all decorated with memories of years gone by and the current year's decorations.

Chili Con Carne

2 1 lb. cans kidney beans (I drain some fluid when expanding recipe)
1 lg. onion, sliced or chopped
1 green pepper, chopped
1 lb. ground beef
1 1 lb. can (2 C.) tomatoes (I've used a variety of kinds, with/without seasoning)
1 8 oz. (1 C.) seasoned tomato sauce
1-1 1/2 Tbsp. chili powder
1 1/2 tsp. salt
1 bay leaf
dash paprika
dash cayenne

1. Brown onion, green pepper, and ground beef in a little hot fat. Drain and put in large pot.

2. Add beans, tomatoes, tomato, sauce and spices.

3. Cover. Simmer 1 1/2 hours. Longer only increases good flavor. I've left it on for several hours.

Notes: The recipe says it will make 6 servings, but I find it usually is good for only 4. Depends on what else is served and when. Multiply 5 times to serve about 20, 7 times to serve 25. If multiplying 6 times, pour off fluid on about 1/2 the beans only be sure to add all the rest of the sauce and fluid from tomatoes. I usually multiply how many ounces of something I need and then buy the largest cans possible to save money and tin. We usually brown the meat, and pour in the beans early the day of the party and then let it simmer all afternoon. I freeze whatever is left over for other meals. As people have brought more appetizers, I've had a little more to freeze for us, but I always make enough for everyone to have plenty, or some to take home as well.

Bountiful Blessings

A blessings party is a great way to give thanks for a new home, renovated kitchen, patio, sun room, etc. We have invited couples who are our closest friends, relatives and the pastor/priest of our church. We all have friends and family we treasure. This is a way to share our gifts and fortune with others.

We create an informal dinner party, usually a buffet supper. The pastor/priest gives a blessing for the new room, etc. All who attend have their picture taken in the new surroundings. What a wonderful way to bring people together!!

The menu usually consists of :
Meat Lasagna
Vegetable Lasagna
Hot Crusty Bread
Green and Mandarin Salad
Wine
Frozen Dessert

Deliciouso!

Celebrate your Heritage Party

Example: Luck of the Irish or Halfway to St. Patrick's Day Party

Our friends with a strong Irish heritage started this tradition more than 20 years ago with a newsletter they mail out around March 17th instead of the traditional holiday letter. This would be the perfect way to let others know about your heritage and the date to mark their calendar for the upcoming party.

The invitation could be in the shape of a shamrock and written in a Gaelic-style font.

Ideas:

The menu consists of:
St. Paddy's Day Pig (possibly a pig roast)
Irish Stew
Green Vegetables
Paddy O' Chips
Key Lime Pie, Irish Whisky Cake
Beer or Sodas for the beverage

The party could include Irish memorabilia, flags, leprechauns, Irish music or other Irish decorations. You could even have someone come dressed as St. Patrick himself and listen to wishes of the guests. The guests could be asked to wear Green attire and bring their Irish sense of humor.

Such a cultural heritage party is a great way to incorporate anyone's culture or background. It could be a fun multi-cultural event.

Valentine Party or Couple's Dinner Party

Cupid strikes again with this event. It's an entertaining way to really get to know couples intimately. We have hosted this party since we were married and have made wonderful friends and lasting friendships as a result.

We invite 5 new couples every year to a casual dinner party. They are each asked to send a baby picture of themselves at least 2 weeks in advance. We also invite our local priest to bless and strengthen our marriages. Each couple must also share the courting experience of how they met as we dine and share conversation.

During the entertainment portion of the evening, each guest is asked to identify each baby picture. There is a prize of homemade chocolates for the male and female winner.

The menu includes:
Cheesy Beefy Strudel
Glazed Baby Carrots and Grapes with Vodka
Rice Pilaf with Mushrooms
Crusty Bread Sticks
Almond Orange Romaine Salad
White Wine
Dessert: Cherries Jubilee with Chocolate Wafer Cookies

Chapter 14 - Hospitality

The Cherries Jubilee is a real hit, elegant and impressive. We serve it with the lights down low and bring it flaming to the table. It's so beautiful and you will receive ooh's and aah's that will last the entire evening. It is about as simple as it comes but your guests will think you fussed for hours.

Cheezy Beefy Strudel
serves 10

2 lb. ground beef
2 T. oil
1 medium onion, chopped
1-2 cloves garlic
1/2 tsp. salt
1/4 tsp. pepper
1-10 oz. frozen chopped broccoli, drained
4 oz. mushrooms, fresh or canned
1/4 lb. Cheddar cheese, grated
4 T. butter
3 T. flour
1 cup milk
1 egg, beaten
1/4 lb. mozzarella cheese, grated
1/2 cup Parmesan cheese, grated
10 phyllo pastry sheets
4 T. butter, melted
Parsley, garnish

Heat oil in skillet. Add onions and sauté until soft. Add ground beef and cook until meat looses its red color. Stir in garlic, salt and pepper. Set aside to cool. Cook the broccoli according to package directions and drain well. Add drained mushrooms. When cool, stir in the cheddar cheese and set aside. Melt 4 T. butter in microwave. Add flour and cook about 1 minute. Pour in the milk and microwave until sauce thickens (about 2 to 3 minutes). Remove and whisk one egg. Microwave for another 1 minute. Set aside to cool slightly. Stir the sauce, mozzarella cheese and Parmesan cheese into the cooled beef mixture. Let cool. (Dish can be prepared ahead to this point.)

Preheat oven to 350 degrees. Lightly grease a large rimmed baking sheet, 10 x 15. Cover work surface with a damp towel. Place 2 phyllo sheets on top of towel with longest edge nearest you. Brush generously with melted butter. Repeat 4 more times, brushing each layer with butter. Spread cooled meat mixture on phyllo. Arrange broccoli mixture in a lengthwise strip along the center of the meat. Using a towel as an aid, roll up phyllo lengthwise. Transfer seam side down to prepared baking sheet and brush with remaining butter. Bake until golden and crisp about 1 hour. Let stand for 10 to 15 minutes before slicing. Arrange slices on serving plate with parsley. (Can be assembled ahead and refrigerated overnight.)
*Phyllo pastry sheets can be found in the frozen food section of grocery stores.

This recipe was one I judged for the Nebraska Beef Cook-off contest and won it 1st place. The recipe comes from Lynda E. Cabela, Chappell, NE

Cherries Jubilee

2 cans (16 oz.) dark sweet cherries, pitted
3 T. cornstarch
1 T. lemon juice
1 tsp. grated lemon rind
3/4 cup sugar
1/2 cup brandy

Into a 2 quart casserole drain cherry syrup. Stir in cornstarch, lemon juice, rind and sugar. Microwave at HIGH 5 to 6 minutes, stirring after 3 minutes, until sauce begins to thicken. Add cherries, stirring well. Measure brandy into glass measure. Microwave at HIGH for 30 seconds. Pour 1 T. heated brandy into metal tablespoon and remaining brandy over top of cherries. Light with match or lighter.

When flame has subsided, serve with vanilla ice cream.

This is a superb and elegant dessert and our guests always rave!

New Year's Eve Jammie Party

Our special friends came up with this idea for New Year's Eve and it was a hit! It's a cold time of year in many parts of the country and curling up next to the fire on New Year's Eve sounds warm and cozy. How about doing that with friends, company workers, or relatives in a party atmosphere?

Instead of dressing up for New Year's, our friends had everyone come to the party dressed in their favorite PJ's to the party, no matter who the guests or what age. Dress in your flannels, night shirt, leopard, or Mother Hubbard gown.

Everyone played Charades, with titles that had a sleepy time theme. Some examples were Sleepless in Seattle, Goodnight Moon, Sleeping with the Enemy and Good Night Irene.

There can be awards given for the following PJs attire:
Most mismatched
Sexiest
Most colorful
Most revealing
Most Play Boy Bunnyish
Boom Chicka Boom Boom award (use your imagination on this one)
Hugh Heffner Award
Most Cindi Lou Who Award
Mother Hen Award
Most Comfortable
Most Original

The menu was entirely breakfast foods of all kinds and flavors:
Orange-Raisin Oatmeal
Belgian Waffles
Egg-Cheese Casserole Bake
Cinnamon Rolls
Variety of Cold Cereals
Fruit Compote
Seasonal Breads, Muffins and Jams
Irish Coffee
Variety of Juices

Belgian Waffles
Makes 60 waffles

All ingredients need to be room temperature.

2.2 lb. flour
5 T. dried yeast
14 oz. butter
4 cups milk
4 cups lite beer or water
8 eggs, separated (egg whites beaten until stiff)
1 pinch of salt

Mix yeast and water (10 tablespoons). Let rest for 5 minutes. Mix flour, yeast mixture, egg yolks, milk and butter. Gradually add beer and fold in beaten egg whites. Let stand at room temperature for 1 hour in a draft free place. Place 1/2 ladle full of batter in hot Belgian waffle iron and cook until golden brown.

Serve with real cream, powdered sugar and berries: strawberries, blueberries, blackberries, etc.

This recipe is from my Belgian friend who makes these for many breakfasts or family events.

To order additional copies of

"Grip, Grin & Greet"
contact
Luann Alemao
Luann Alemao and Associates
2317 Country Lane
Cedar Falls, IA 50613
319-266-8021

email: l.alemaoassoc@cfu.net

www.LAandA.com